Marriage is a

For Better Word

by Diane Pfeifer
Illustrations by Clark Taylor
Published by Strawberry Patch, Atlanta, Georgia

ISBN: 1-887987-00-2
Library of Congress Number: 95-74709

Published by: Strawberry Patch
P.O. Box 52404
Atlanta, GA 30355-0404
404-261-2197

Editor: Diane Pfeifer
Cover Design: Paula Chance, Atlanta, GA
Interior Design: Jeff Justice

This book celebrates the marriage of

_____

and

_____

on

_____

From

_____

for Richer

for Poorer

"Look for a sweet person. Forget rich."

Estee Lauder

in Health

for Truer

for Falser

for Trendy

for Happier

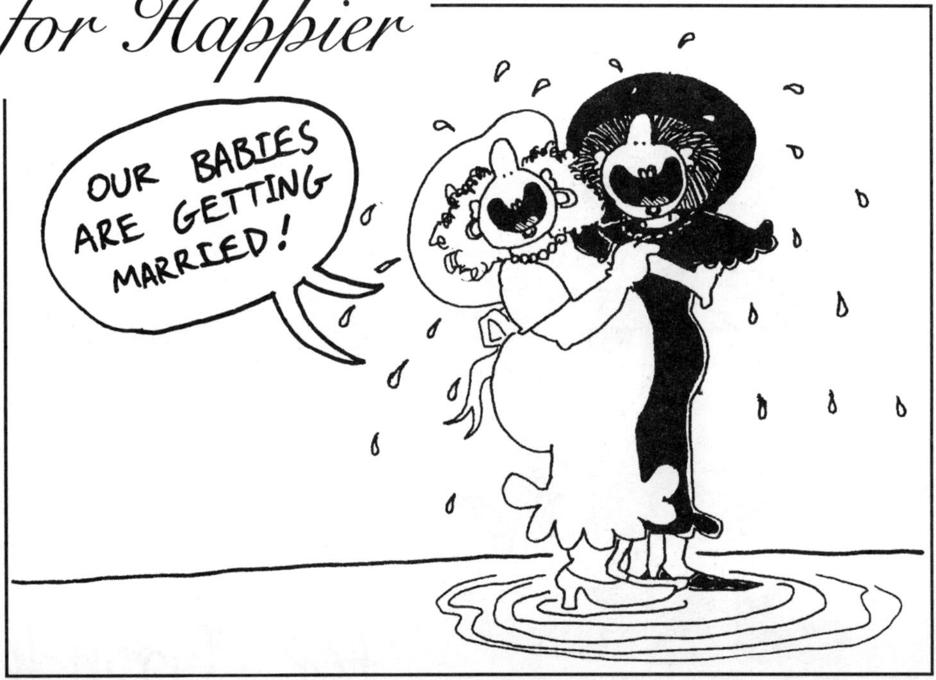

for Sadder

*"Basically my wife is immature.
I'd be at home in the bath
and she'd come in and sink my boats."*

Woody Allen

for Whiter

for Blacker

for Thinner

for Hi-Tech

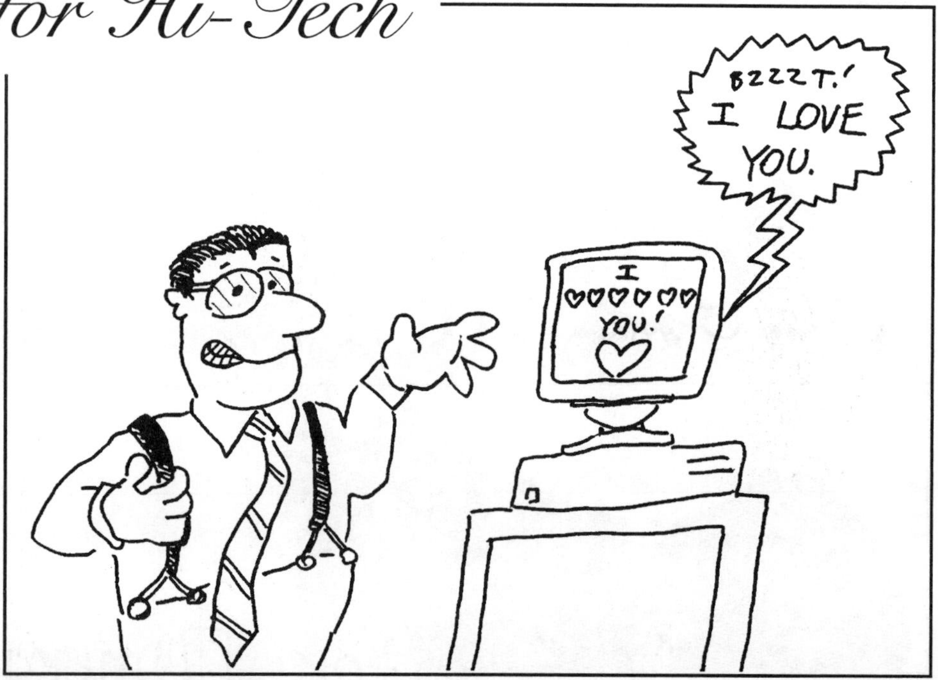

"*Love conquers all.*"

Virgil

for Down

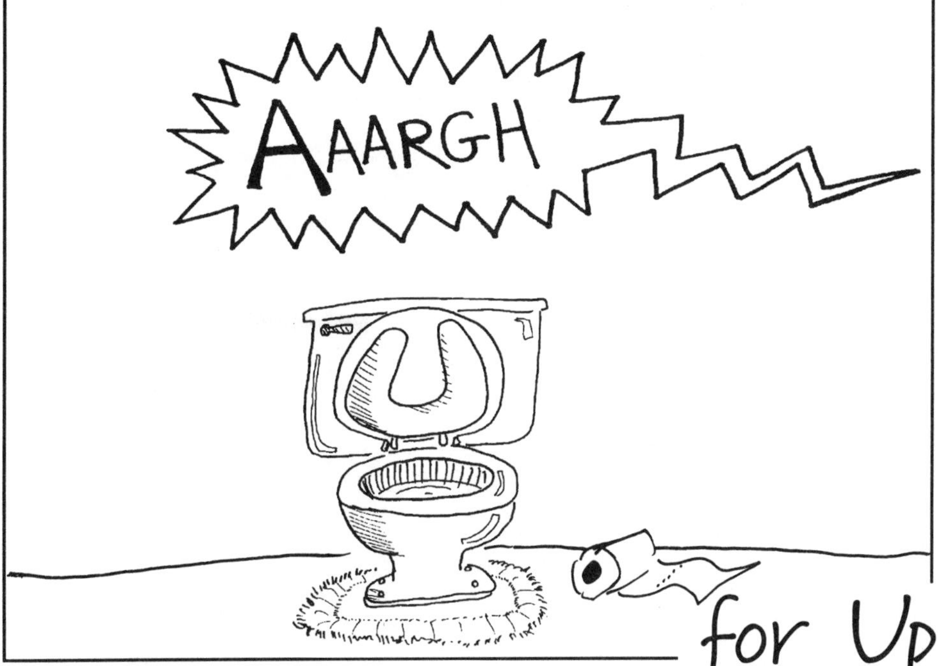

for Up

for Accepting

for Returning

for Shinier

" All the world

loves a lover."

Ralph Waldo Emerson

for Conflict

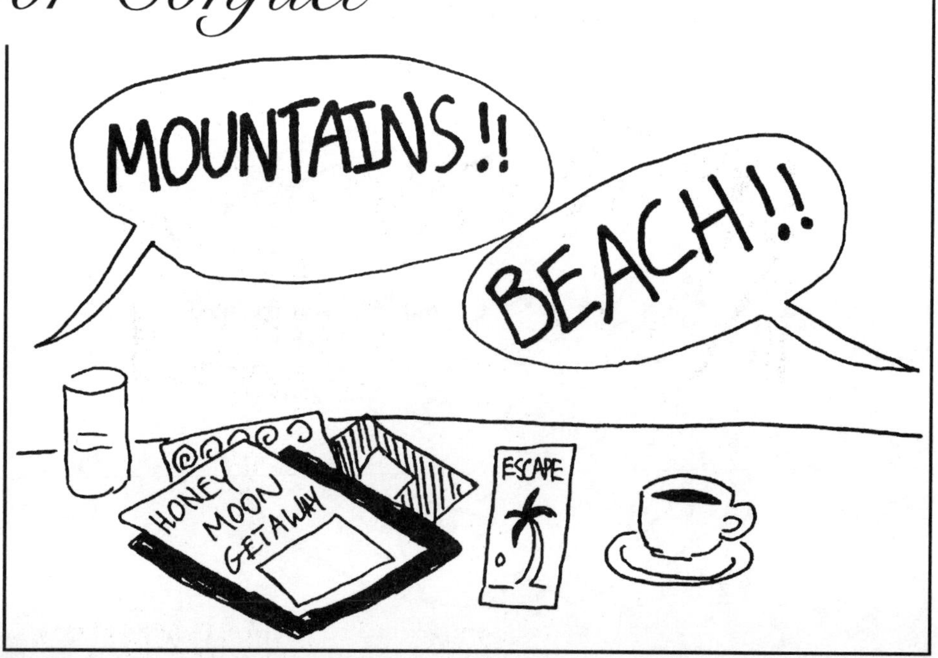

for Compromise

for Colder

for Crowded

"A successful man is one who makes more money than his wife can spend. A successful woman is one who can find such a man."

Lana Turner

for Earlier

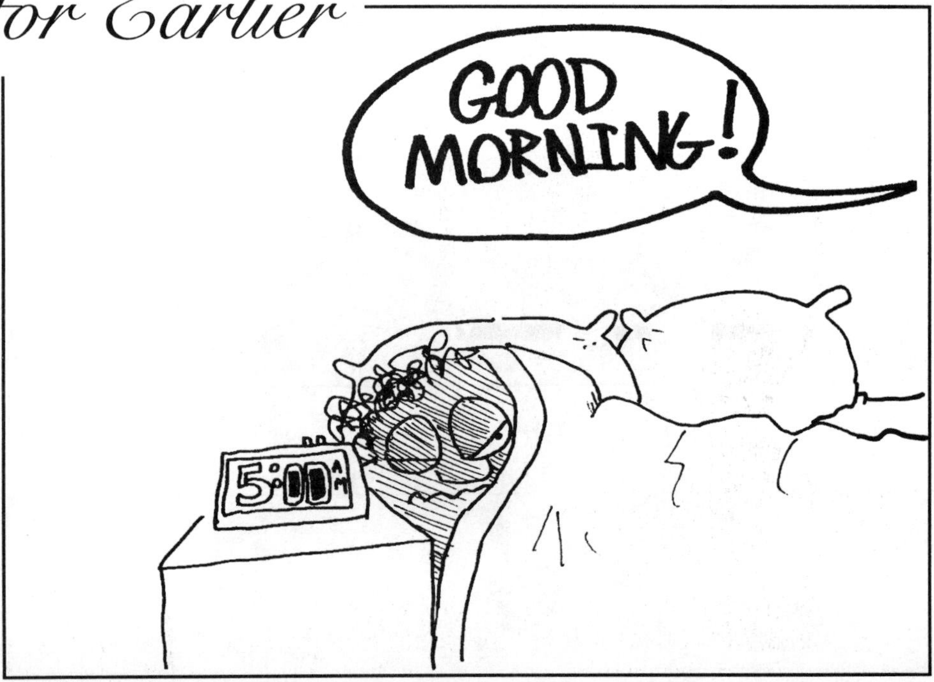

for Later

for Thrifty

for Bigger

for Smaller

" An archaeologist is the best husband any woman can have; the older she gets, the more he is interested in her."

Agatha Christie

for Higher

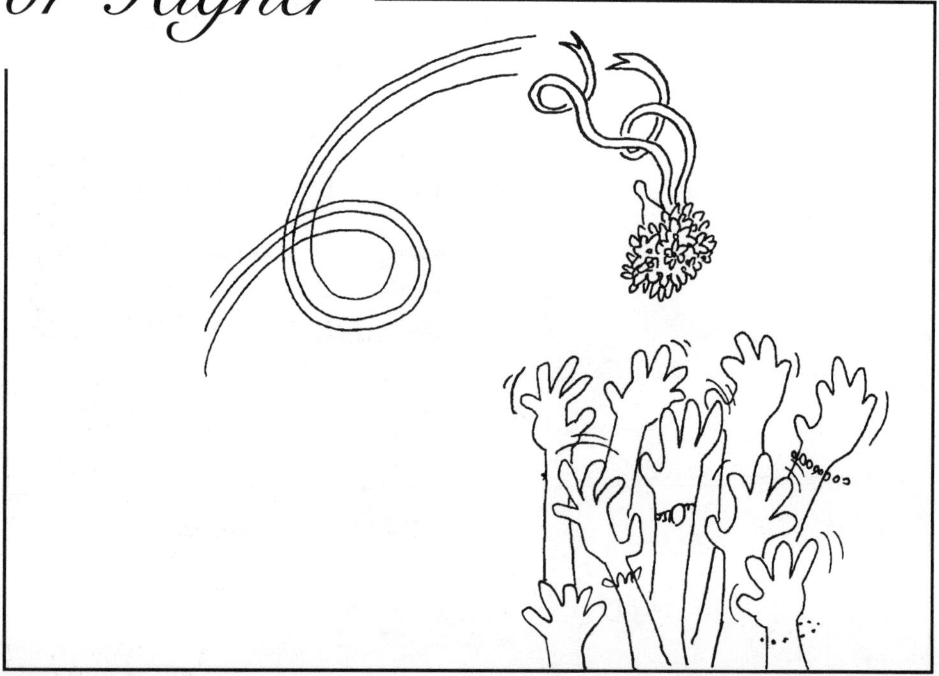

for Lower

for Lighter

for Darker

for Walking

for Running

" A happy marriage is
a long conversation
which always seems too short."

Andre Maurois, French writer

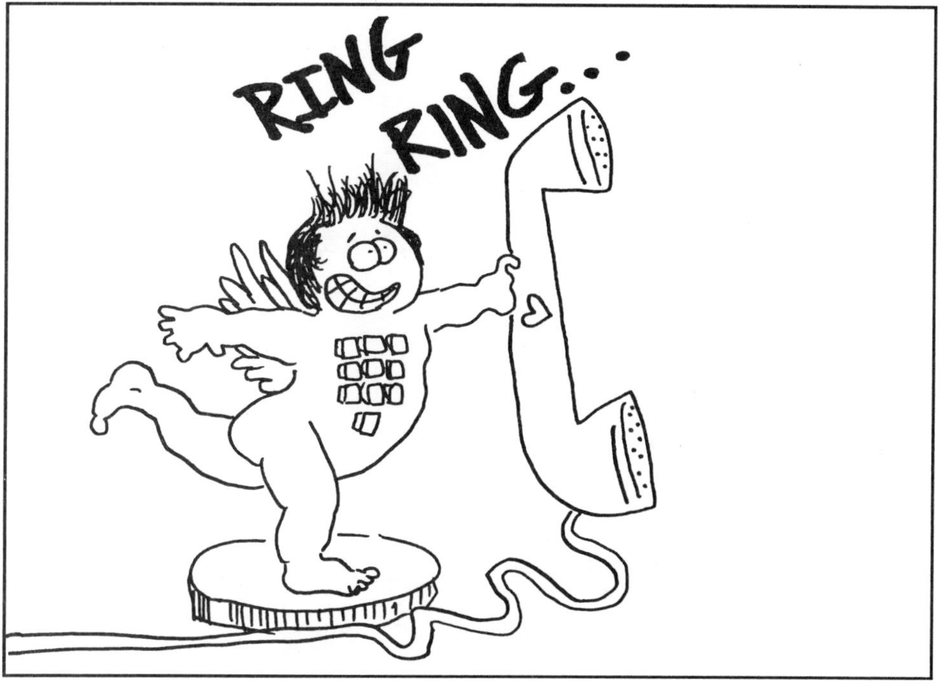
RING
RING...

for Tighter

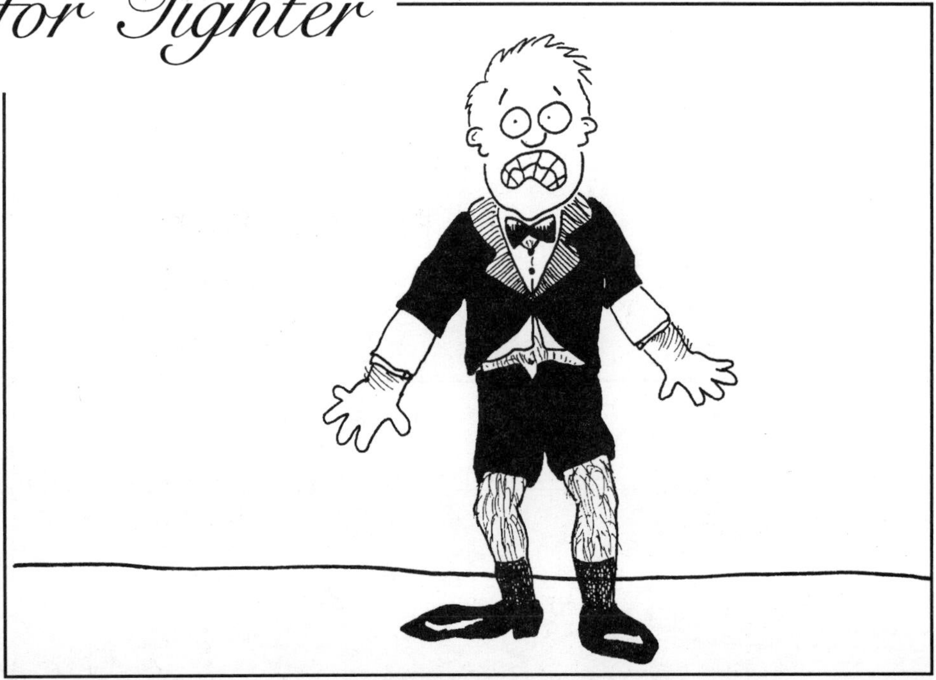

for Looser

for Forgetting

for Stronger

for Weaker

*"If you want to be loved,
love and be lovable."*

Ben Franklin

for Tasteful

for Tacky

for Obeying

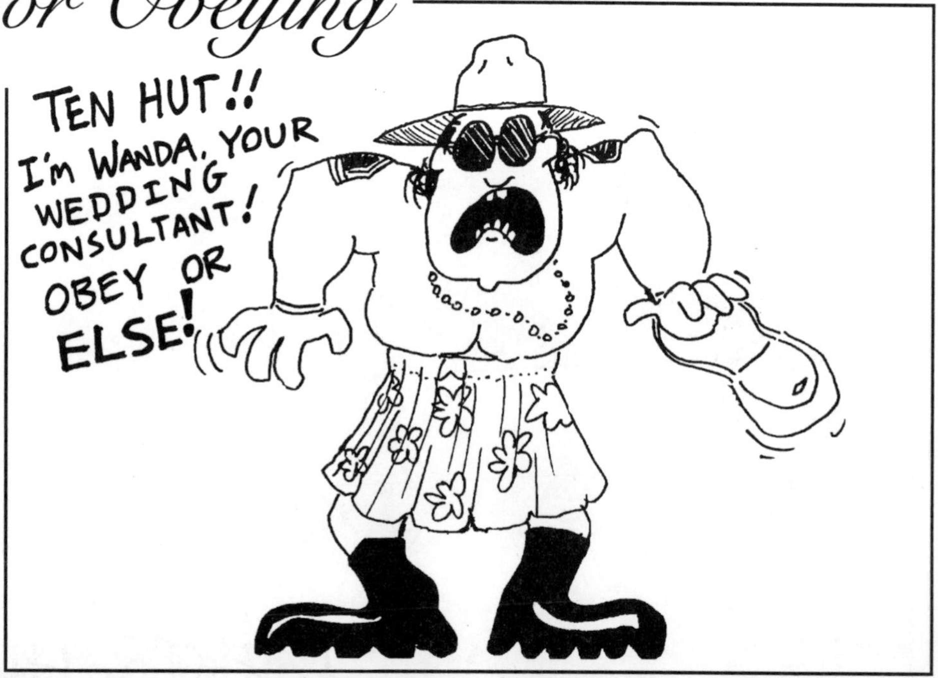

for Disobeying

for Even

" Marriage is not just spiritual communion and passionate embraces. Marriage is also three meals a day and remembering to take out the trash."

Joyce Brothers

for Longer

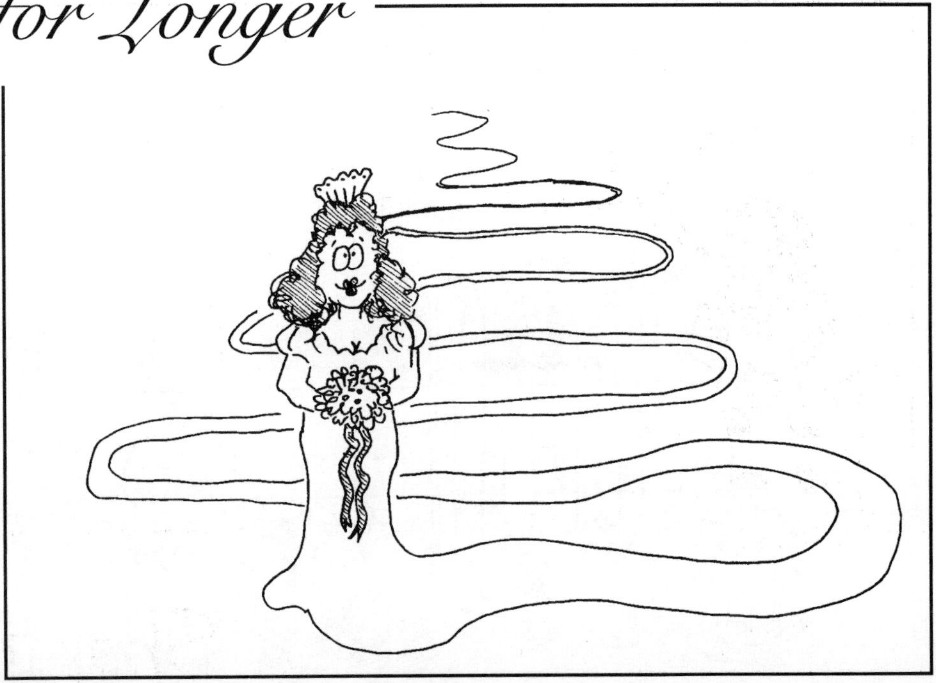

for Shorter

for Softer

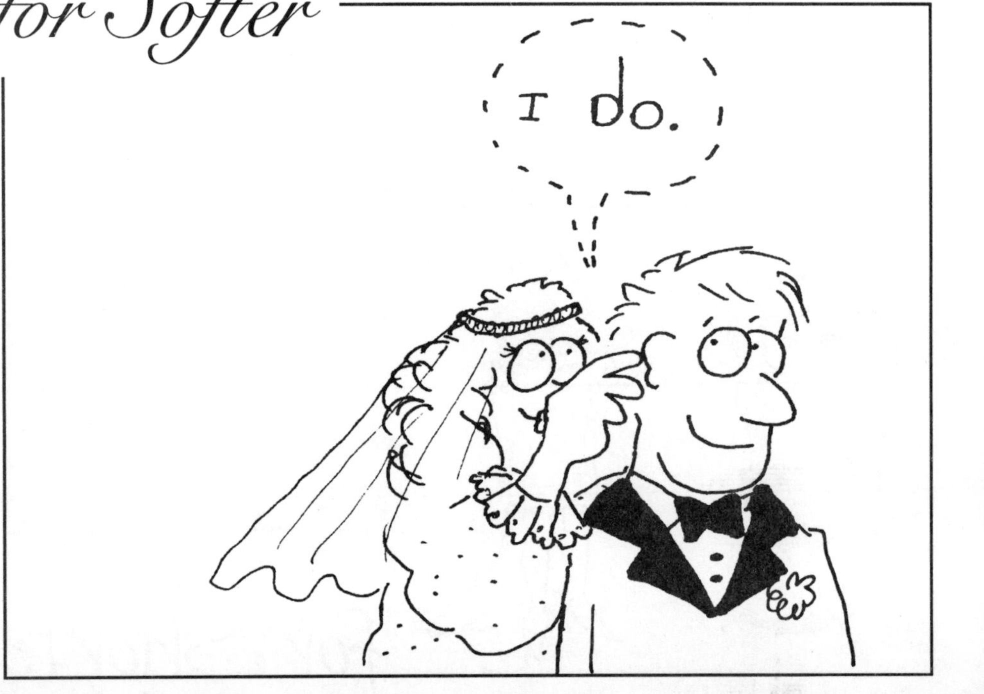

for Louder

"Every woman needs a man to discover her."

Charlie Chaplin

for Bluer

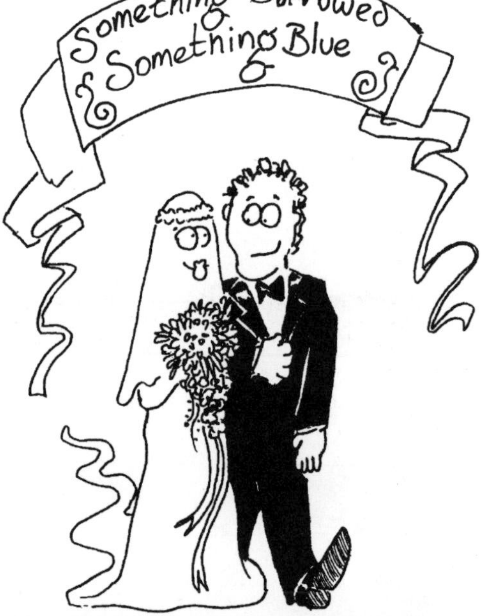

for Disharmony

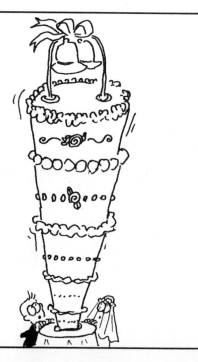

for Flatter

*"The love we give away
is the very love we keep."*

Elbert Hubbard

for Slower

for Faster

for Above

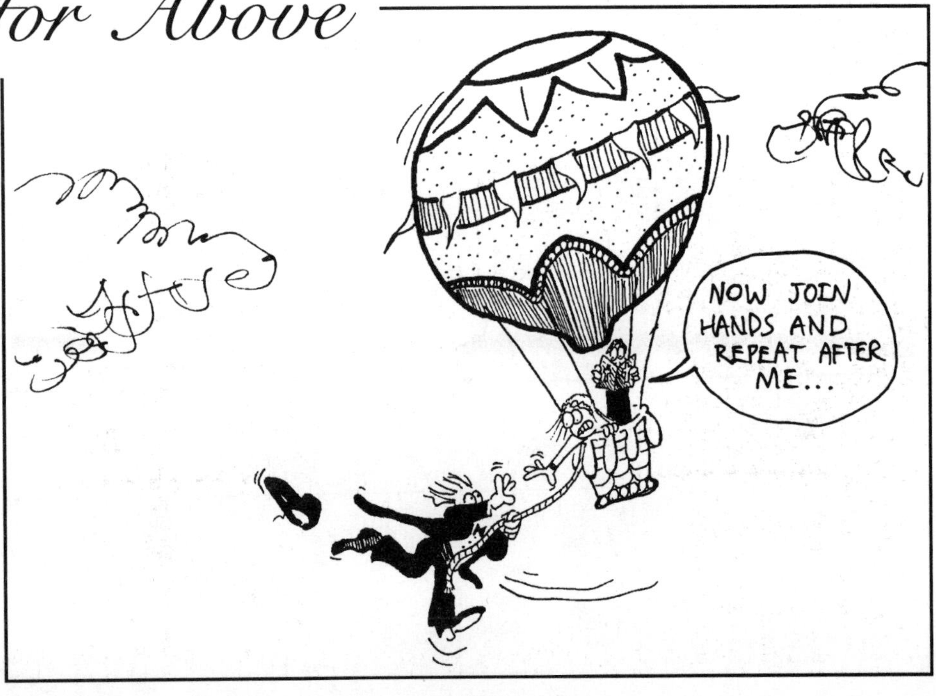

for Below

for Blacker

for Grayer

"It was so cold I almost got married."

Shelley Winters

for Alike

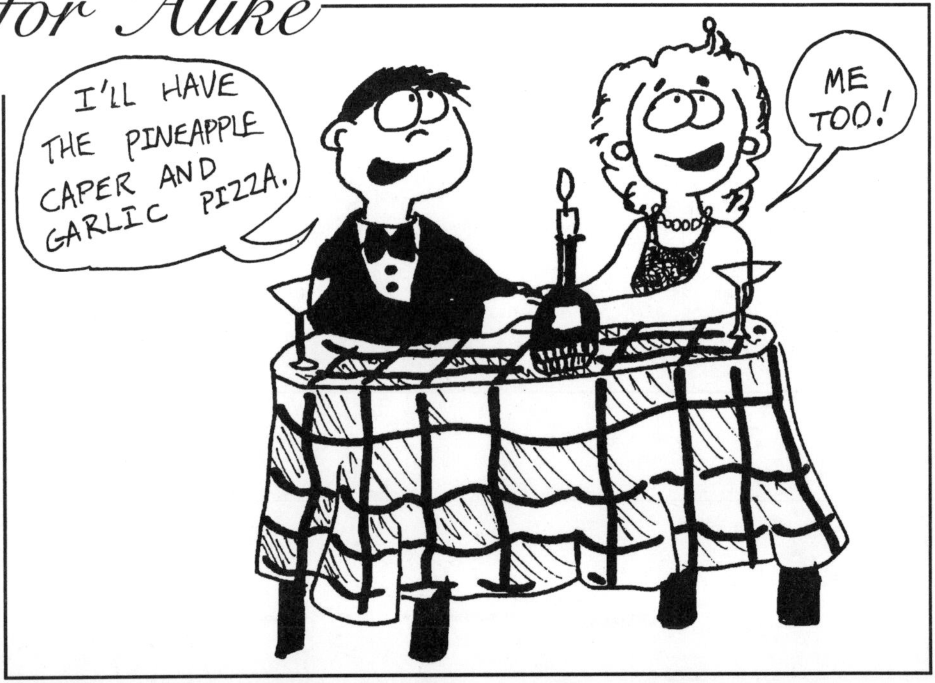

for Different

for Separate

for Clingy

for Out

for In

"The great secret of a successful marriage is to treat all disasters like incidents and none of the incidents like disasters."

Harold Nicholson, British politician

UH... UM... HONEY? YOU KNOW THAT LITTLE BOTTLE OF PERFUME ON THE MANTEL THAT YOU REALLY LIKE TO WEAR?...
LE EXPENSE

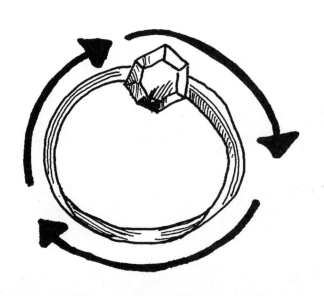

for Squarer

for Tossing

_____ for Gathering

*" Marriage is an edifice
that must be rebuilt every day."*

Andre Maurois, French writer

for Now

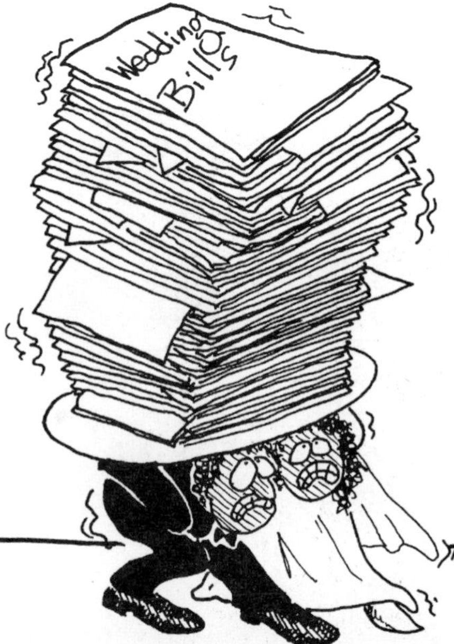

for Later

for Confident

"*The first duty of love is to listen.*"

Paul Tillich

for Wetter

for Drier

for Sneaky

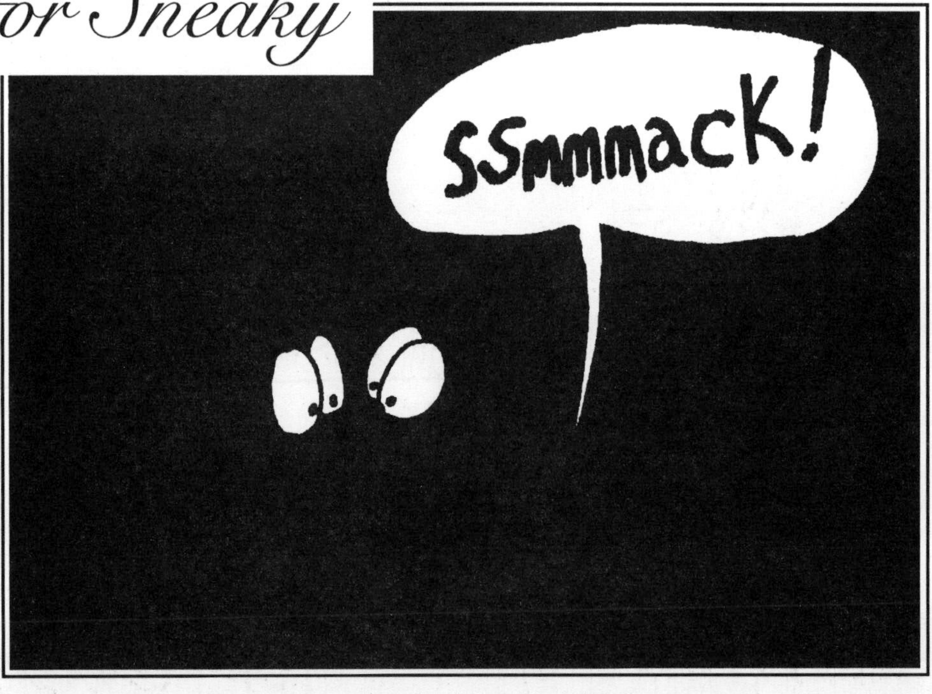

for Open

"There is no more lovely, friendly and charming relationship, communion or longing than a good marriage."

Martin Luther

For Ever...